I'M WITH YOU

ATTEMPT THE IMPOSSIBLE, BECAUSE

THAT'S THE ONLY WAY YOU MAKE IT

POSSIBLE.

KOTARO UMEDA

To mom, dad, and my brother, thank you

CONTENTS

INTRODUCTION

------------- ❦❧ -------------

We don't know what people hide behind their smiles or what they have been through that have got them to where they are today. I'm not trying to change people's lives, but I believe it's my duty to use my platform to speak on behalf of others to motivate them regularly. We're all human beings, in that we all experience anxiety, the loss of a loved one, the need to feel loved, and much more. Experiencing life can be difficult and may even seem impossible at times. However, I want people to understand that they're never alone in the fight because *I'm With You.* My name is Kotaro Umeda, and I was born in Tokyo, Japan to a loving family. My mother, Julie Umeda, was a successful dentist in Japan, and my father, Yuji Umeda, was a successful orthopedic surgeon in Japan. I have an older brother, Yuta Umeda, who is currently enrolled in a medical school, trying to follow my father's footsteps of becoming a doctor. Family means everything to me because we were constantly moving throughout my childhood. Although I'm Japanese, I mostly grew up in American cities, such as Albuquerque, New Mexico, and Cleveland, Ohio. In my 21 years of life, I've experienced some unimaginable events as well as some normal life events, just like everyone else. There were times when I thought I couldn't get through this phase or times when I thought it was necessary for me to give up on my ambitions. Right now, I'm a professional soccer player in Brazil. It's important to live life with a purpose and passion because we only get one chance. This book includes some of the most important life lessons that have helped me become who I am today. Each chapter provides a lesson I learned from my personal experience that has changed my life tremendously. If by writing this book, I can change the life of one human being, I know it was worth it. Mahatma Gandhi once said "as one person, I cannot change the world, but I can change the world of one person".

CHAPTER 1:

———————— ❦❧❦❧ ————————

EVERYTHING HAPPENS FOR A

REASON

It is natural to become upset or frustrated when things don't go our way. But what if we changed our perspective from "why me?" to "try me" and realized that everything happens for a reason? With the expectation of twins in early January 1995, my mother, my father, and my brother were beyond excited to have a bigger family in the household. Ever since my older brother Yuta was born, he always dreamed of having a younger brother, someone he could play with. God had responded to my brother's prayers by providing my family twin boys on January 12, 1995. What seemed like a dream year for the Umeda family was just the beginning of the toughest year of our lives. The twin boys both passed away immediately due to health complications, each weighing only 2,000 grams. My family did not know how to react, as their hearts were shattered within minutes. Just as when it seemed like the Umeda family was getting bigger, it had actually gotten smaller. The pain of losing twin boys stayed in my parents' hearts until 1998, when I was born. The greatest miracle is that I was born weighing 4,000 grams, the exact weight of the two twin boys who had been taken to heaven in 1995. My mother still, to this day, believes that I have the life of the twins and they will forever protect me as they are always with me. Everything really does happen for a reason.

Two months after the tragic incident in 1995, another trial struck our family. First and foremost, I want to let you guys know that my brother was someone who did not care about his appearance as a child. He would wear any clothes he found and always wore Velcro shoes, since they were easier to put on. But as my mother was getting ready to take my brother to preschool and go to work on Monday morning, on March 20, 1995, my brother refused to wear Velcro shoes, insisting on wearing shoes with laces. In confusion and frustration because she might miss her subway to work, my mother rushed to tie my brother's shoes. However, my brother refused to walk outside unless she re-tied them. As my mother's frustration increased, my brother begged her once more to re-tie his shoes. My mother rushed to the subway station with my brother, hoping to catch the Hibiya Subway Line at 8:14 AM in Tsukiji Station. Just as she arrived at the station, she noticed that the entrance was blocked off and multiple ambulance trucks and police cars were surrounding the station. Confused, my mother still went down the stairs as she was desperate to get to work on time. As she reached the station, she saw multiple bodies lying on the ground. In shock, she rushed back up to be informed that there was a terrorist attack in the Hibiya Subway Line, the same exact one my mother was supposed to get on. The only thing that stopped my mother from getting on the subway with a dozen fatalities was my brother begging my mother to re-tie his shoes. If it wasn't for my brother and his shoes, my mother would not be here, or in this case, I would not be here.

Everything really does happen for a reason.

People may say it was luck, or a miracle, but I know that everything happens for a reason. What God has planned for us is much bigger than anything we could ever imagine. The instant reaction we have in times of trials and tribulations is irrelevant to the result that the process will bring us. In times of difficulty, we don't understand why or what is happening to us because our instant reaction is rejection of fear and pain; however, beyond the pain and fear lies a whole new level of strength and opportunity. One must stay optimistic in times of need to realize that everything that happens in our lives happens for a reason. Right after the Sarin Gas Attack in Tokyo that killed 12 individuals and injured 1,050 people, my mother was very sick for weeks. Yet, she decided to go visit the cemetery of a friend who had passed away in the attack in honor and respect. All of a sudden, after her visit, her sickness was gone. I realize how precious life is because without the passing of my twin brothers and my brother's dislike of his shoes, I would not be here. I also realize how easily life can be taken away from us. Within seconds, even when you simply get ready for work, have the same breakfast you have been having for years, and catch the same exact Hibiya Subway Line, you can be killed by a group of terrorists whose intentions are to separate the world.

For some of us, our trials and tribulations may be bigger or smaller than what my family has gone through. We all have different experiences in life, as well as different perspectives. However, it is not about the size of our struggles, but how we react to our struggles, that define who we are. Whether your struggles may be a murdered family member, a terrorist attack in a subway, or a tough breakup, it is important to realize that everything really does happen for a reason. Being redirected is a blessing, because you come to the realization that the path you were on was not the right path for you and the redirection will take you to where you need to be. I didn't always have this perspective. When things didn't go the way I wanted them to, I used to get upset and question myself. However, without the events in my life, I wouldn't be where I am today, literally and metaphorically. When one door is closed, another door is opened. When we go through struggles, an opportunity to become a better version of us lies beyond the struggles. Of course, creating this perspective is not easy, it takes time and lots of practice, but living your life dwelling on every struggle is unimaginable. Constantly being upset with yourself for the misfortunes that you go through cannot help you become the best version of yourself because you will constantly become complacent with no progress. The next time you encounter a defeat, whether that may be spilling coffee on your shirt or losing a job, come to the realization that everything happens for a reason and your redirection will lead to a positive outcome with a positive mindset.

CHAPTER 2:

——————— ⚜ ———————

FOREVER LOVED

"Everybody dies, but not

everybody lives."

Unfortunately, death is a part of our lives, whether it is the loss of a family member, a close friend, a teammate, or a classmate. The closest person I have lost in my life was my grandma, who passed away due to a sudden heart attack on April 29, 1998. I wasn't physically close to her as I was only 2 months old when she passed away, but my spiritual connection with my grandma goes far beyond imaginable measures. My mother and father tell me multiple stories about my grandma that I adore, but the one that I love the most is that she was the first person I had ever smiled at, while in her arms.

Faith sees the invisible, feels the intangible, and achieves the impossible. Even though I never got to spend time on Earth with my grandma, I know she will protect me and love me for as long as I breathe because that's who she is. Even though I can't trace my grandma, I trust her because she raised my father, my hero, to be who he is.

My grandma didn't have an easy life raising my father and my aunt. Although my grandparents shared tremendous loving moments together, they couldn't always live under the same roof. They were so poor that my grandpa was forced to go work in other far away cities for months, which was devastating for my grandma and their two children. But my grandma never gave up on family and raised both my father and his sister as a single parent in the household, which is amazing. As my father watched his parents struggle to put food on the table, he inherited their tremendous work ethic, which I learned from my father as well. When you see someone willing to sacrifice their life for you, it shows you the true meaning of love. Although my father's family was torn apart physically, the thing that kept them together was love, which was also the only thing they needed.

Everybody dies, but not everybody lives.

My grandma certainly served her time on Earth with tremendous love and care.

"Service to others is the rent you pay

for your room here on Earth."

-Muhammad Ali

When you lose someone so close to you, it is beyond difficult to get back up on your feet. My family struggled a lot trying to live day to day without the one person we relied on so much. There is a famous Portuguese phrase,

"Tudo Passa," which means that everything passes, all good things and bad things will be healed by time. Nothing in this world lasts forever, which may be a blessing or a burden. The scars that were left on my family after the loss of my grandma were healed by time. Although she will remain in our hearts forever, we know that she is in a better place, watching over us. There is a model called the Kubler-Ross model, more commonly known as the five stages of grief, that helps us monitor the progression of our emotional states. The five stages are denial, anger, bargaining, depression, and acceptance. My family's initial reaction to my grandmother's death was denial, partly because her heart attack was random and we didn't expect it. It is certainly difficult to have to believe that someone you love so much is physically gone at first. I personally don't think my family went through the anger stage, as far as I know, or maybe they try to cover it up since it was such a dark period for them.

However, my family dealt with bargaining and depression by changing the environment we were surrounded by, because one must change their environment before the environment changes them. When I was 4 months old, 2 months after the death of my grandma, my family decided to move to Albuquerque, New Mexico. The new environment and completely different culture allowed us to clear our minds of sadness and depression, allowing us to meet new people and create lifelong friendships. After spending two lovely years in New Mexico, my family decided it was time to move back to Tokyo and sort of "get back to reality." I think this was our acceptance stage and realization that our grandma is physically gone and will remain in our hearts forever. People say that the five stages of grief may take up to 6 months, but it took our family over 2 years, and that's what is so important. Nobody in this world experiences events in life the same way, we have different thoughts and different emotions.

Our society attempts to declare what is right and what is wrong for all of us when, in reality, every one of us are made in our own unique way and we experience life differently. Instead of trying to hide our pain and fear, it is important to embrace the struggle because we never know who we may inspire on our journey. It is okay to take all the time you need and get all the help you need because you are the one walking in your own shoes, nobody else. It took over 2 years for my family to accept the loss of my grandma, but *tudo passa*.

There is no right or wrong way to deal with the death of a loved one, just as there is no right or wrong way to love someone. Receiving help, embracing the pain, and taking all the time you need was how my family coped with the loss of our grandma.

CHAPTER 3:

———— ❧ ✦❀✦ ❧ ————

EVERY PARENT'S NIGHTMARE

"Nobody can relate to the pain, unless

they have gone through it themselves."

Sometimes, life's greatest teaching moments are the most painful ones. One of the saddest things to hear as a parent is that your son or daughter is being bullied at school. Although I can't speak on behalf of the parent's (since I am not yet a parent), I have been on the opposite end, as I was bullied throughout school. Being bullied destroys everything, your self-confidence, your happiness, your excitement, and most importantly, your willingness to live.

As a preschooler, I thought that death was possibly better than living. It is absolutely unacceptable for any human being to ever think that, let alone a 4-year-old. The scariest part of it all is that I was not only bullied by students, but by the teachers as well.

I cried every morning, holding on to the door-knob of our living room and refusing to go to preschool. My mother used to force me to leave the house with her as she thought I was just upset that I wasn't going to be with her for the day. As weeks went by, my self-confidence faded, as well as my willingness to live. My preschool celebrated our birthdays where they allowed our mothers or fathers to come and "enjoy" the day with us. I couldn't wait for my 5th birthday to come so I could be with my mother during school and hold her hand during those frightening days.

Birthdays for your kids are supposed to be filled with joy and happiness, but my mother's heart was completely shattered on mine. As my mother and I entered the building on February 15, 2003, she was confused to see why I stood at the door watching every other student grab their name tag and walk into the classroom. When asked why I waited to be the last student to walk in, I told my mother, "I don't know how to read Japanese so the only way I know to grab my name tag is to wait for my name to be the last one on the table." I could still remember the look of shock in my mother's eyes as she rushed to my teacher to ask why she couldn't help me. The teacher simply responded, "It's not our fault your child doesn't know how to read." During lunch, while every other student sat together, having fun and enjoying their meal, my mother was crushed to see me eating alone in silence, hunched over the lunch that she had packed for me. As she questioned me, "Kota, why don't you eat with your friends? Why are you eating alone?" I answered, "The teacher doesn't let me sit with other people because I can't speak Japanese good." I had never seen my mother look so heartbroken in my life, but I, myself, was also defeated and hopeless. The day only got worse as recess came and every other student was enjoying their free time and playing outside. I was forced by my teachers to complete the task of getting to a certain height on the swing during my so-called "free time." I was never taught how to swing on the swing set, and I failed miserably every single day. As my mother watched me struggle, she questioned my teacher as to why I had to do this. She replied, "It's a skill set that every student here needs to know before they can go to recess." I had never seen my mother's heart shatter like this, and without any further questions, she grabbed my hand and rushed to the principal's office. As the principal told my mother, "These are all basic skill sets your child needs to learn or he will accomplish nothing in life," we left the preschool on my birthday heartbroken and defeated.

I have never seen anyone apologize so much to me, especially my mother. I can still remember her shaking and holding back tears as she constantly repeated, "I am so sorry, Kota. I love you so much, I promise." We instantly changed schools, and our future seemed optimistic.

I never blamed my mother or father for putting me through such a difficult time, because it was not their fault and they were busy putting a roof over my head, food on the table, and clothes on my back, which I will forever be thankful for. Being bullied was a blessing in disguise for me because it made me stronger than I could have ever imagined. I had to go through the dark times to cherish the good times, and without the experiences I had in school, who is to say whether I would have become the man I am now.

The same boy who was told by his preschool teachers that he was not going to accomplish anything in life is the same boy who became a professional soccer player and is pursuing a career in public speaking to inspire others. We are limitless. Other people will only tell you what you can't do, and if you listen to others, we will accomplish minimal things in life. Even through the darkest times when no one believes in us, we must believe in ourselves. Bullying is something no student should ever have to go through, but in reality, we will never live a life where every school is bully-free, because it happens. As a parent, you never know what your son or daughter is hiding behind their smiles, so I beg you to listen to them, listen to their screams, listen to their conversations, but most importantly, listen to their whispers because the few times when we speak up, our voices shake. Believe your child, believe him or her because even though they may be lying, there will always be some truth behind their stories. Too often, bullied students are isolated from their friends, classmates, teachers, and most importantly, their family. Protect your child, support your child, and most importantly, love your child unconditionally, because they are the greatest miracle in your life.

CHAPTER 4:

———— ❧❧❧❧❧ ————

HOMES

"Home is not a place...

it's a feeling."

It may take people no time or it may take people their entire life to realize that life's greatest gift is family. Growing up, I never had a consistent "home" as my family moved from country to country, from apartment to apartment, with the very little money we had. For me, home was wherever my family was, because that's where I wanted to be, surrounded by the people who loved me unconditionally. For many of us, home is a certain location where a family has created so many memories, met so many people they adore, and lived a neighborhood that never changes.

I was born in Tokyo, Japan, but my family moved to Albuquerque, New Mexico when I was 4 months old because of my dad's work and to change the environment we were in (Chapter 2). My mom always tells me the story of how she gave me sleeping pills so I was knocked out and didn't annoy the other passengers on the plane. We lived in multiple apartments and motels in New Mexico, to the point where we didn't have a consistent address for our grandparents to send us packages. We fell in love with New Mexico; the weather, the views, the people, the Native American culture, it was all beautiful. But after two years of living in the United States, my family decided it was time to move back to Tokyo. I spent a lot of time struggling in Japan because I couldn't speak Japanese and was a little different from the "normal" kids. We lived in two different apartments in Tokyo, both very close to one another but very different in rent. I remember playing soccer in the parking lot with my brother and climbing trees in the backyard. Day by day, I adored Japan, the culture, the food, the people, the city, it all just fascinated me. Just as I started to become comfortable with the neighborhood and started making friends in school, my parents gave me heartbreaking news. We were moving to the United States again. As a first grader, I was confused by the news, but my brother, who was in fifth grade at the time, knew exactly what was going on and was so furious that it looked as if he was fighting with his life to stay. On September 2004, my family moved to Cleveland, Ohio, for my father's work. I remember arriving at the airport with my mother and my brother as my father pulled up in a broken-down Honda Civic. The ride to the hotel was awfully quiet and sad because we missed Japan, and we knew this was going to be an entirely different lifestyle. Just as I was getting used to the Japanese culture and language, I was forced to surround myself with another different culture and language. School was a nightmare for me. I never spoke, and I was always hiding behind other students so I wouldn't be seen. I felt unimportant and unwanted by a lot of people, because we were the minority of the country. These events allowed me to become even closer to my family, and the only thing I looked forward to was Saturday, when my dad, my brother, and I would go to my elementary school's soccer field and play soccer for hours, just the three of us, and afterward, my mother would always make us the best food in the world. We moved three times during my time at Cleveland, and I will forever cherish the memories I had in each of my homes.

My parents weren't educationally strict like the stereotypical "Asian parents," but were rather loving. I personally believe that strict parents raise sneaky kids, and from my experience, kids who had very strict parents are the ones who abuse drugs and alcohol in college when they get their own freedom. It is important to be strict, but I also believe that it is more important to be reasonable to your kids. My mom always told me, "Learn from the mistakes of others, you can't make them all yourself" and this has stuck with me forever.

I grew up in a small town in Cleveland called Mayfield. It was a nice place, but if you got caught up in the wrong group of people, you could get yourself into serious trouble. I've had friends who were shot, committed suicide, dropped out of school, overdosed on heroin, killed, locked up in jail, and much more. But my parents always made sure I stayed away from the streets and focused on my dream, which was to become a professional soccer player. No matter where life took me, be it was Tokyo, Albuquerque, Cleveland, Louisville, Akron, or Joinville, I always had three things with me, God, family, and soccer, the only things I needed.

Although growing up was tough, since we were constantly moving and never had a stable house, I look back at how far I have come and realize how blessed I am. My parents are both very ambitious people who will always attempt the impossible. Everything was set for my family; my mother was a successful dentist and my father was a successful orthopedic surgeon in Japan, living in one of the best cities in the world, Tokyo. But the one thing that made them leave their luxurious lifestyle to start over in Cleveland was the love they had for us. The lack of freedom and strict educational system in Japan was not something my parents believed in.

As a first-generation minority in a politically disputed nation, the odds were against us. We weren't supposed to make it out. My mother went from working 9am to 6pm in the crowded city of Tokyo to being a stay-at-home mother taking care of her two little boys. I remember the day my father got the result of his medical exam. He did not pass. Sitting in our tiny apartment in Mayfield, my mother told him, "Honey, we're already in debt. You can't become a doctor here, and we're all suffering. Let's go home to Tokyo, it's okay, we tried."

"Nobody is taller than the last man standing."

But my father never gave up. Today, the first-generation immigrant who "wasn't supposed to make it" is a successful doctor at one of the most famous hospitals in the world, the Cleveland Clinic, is happily married to a successful dental assistant in Cleveland, and is the father to a successful medical student and a professional soccer player.

I learned one of the most important life lessons growing up thanks to my family, who have been with me through everything. A lot of people in life want change but do not want to change, meaning they want to see a difference in the world but don't want to be the difference themselves. I learned that to make any dreams or ambitions come true, you must become comfortable being uncomfortable. I was put into many uncomfortable situations physically and mentally as my family was constantly moving and I was forced to go to multiple different schools. However, I naturally became so comfortable being in uncomfortable situations that I feel untouchable today. I feel as if I can conquer anything I set my mind to, because, in reality, I can. The next time you are forced into an uncomfortable situation, train your mind to stay calm by breathing slowly, and simply understand that if you can overcome this uncomfortable environment, you will become that much stronger. As long as you have the right mindset, you can overcome any obstacle.

CHAPTER 5:

———— ❧~✦~❧ ————

FIGHT THE FIGHT

"Fight as if your life depends on it,

because it does."

There are certain things in life that you never imagine happening to you or your family; some things you thought you would only see in movies or happen to other people. For my family, that unimaginable event was cancer. Just like everybody else, my mother had her annual breast cancer screening, which was a yearly routine for her. On April 21, 2010, my mother received a letter from the Cleveland Clinic that was a little different from the usual letters she received from them. The letter stated, "You have breast cancer. Please seek immediate treatment."

I came home from school that day and the house was awfully quiet. There were no snacks, no "Hi Kota, how was school?" from my mom, nothing. In confusion, I walked through the house and noticed the door of my parents' bedroom closed. As I cracked open the door, I saw my mother crying alone. I was scared, because I had never seen her cry. When I slowly approached her, I asked, "What's wrong, Mom?" and she showed me the letter that had diagnosed her as a cancer patient. My heart was shattered. I couldn't believe that something like this could actually happen to someone so close to you, and as a 12-year-old, I wasn't educated enough about cancer to understand the possibility of life. There are certain words or phrases you never want to hear, and this was certainly one of them. So many thoughts rushed through my head,

"Is my mom going to die? What am I going to do without my mom? How long does she have to live?"

Of course, my father tried to comfort me by saying, "Mom will be okay, she'll just be a little sick for a while," but I knew of the severity of cancer and how terrifying it is. Day by day, I was worried I was going to lose my mother, because my close friend had lost his mother 3 years previously to the same disease.

On June 7, 2010, my mother had her surgery. Although I wanted to be next to her through it all, my father didn't let me skip school that day, probably because he didn't want me to see how weak my mother was going to be. I could not function properly in school that day, crying and praying in the bathroom stall every hour. My father told me that her surgery was successful, but she was going to spend the night at the hospital because she was in serious pain. She came home the next day, but she couldn't walk. I thought to myself, "Did the surgery really go well? My mother looks like she stepped closer towards death than life." I was beyond terrified to see someone so strong become that weak, and my heart was very heavy. My mother was not only fighting for her life, but she was fighting for us.

As she started her recovery process, I spent every possible second next to her, talking to her and being in her presence. Outside of love, the strongest word in the American dictionary is hope, and being with her gave me hope. If the pain eased enough for her to be able to sleep, I would sit next to her in dead silence, praying to God that her sleep was not permanent and that she was going to wake up.

Day by day, my mother became stronger and stronger and it was one of the greatest blessings in my life. Today, my mother is a cancer survivor who works as a dental assistant in Cleveland, Ohio, and is stronger than ever. Although cancer tried to break our family apart, it only brought us closer. The love only grew and our faith only got stronger.

Blessing in disguise...

Seeing someone I love fight for their life created an intrinsic motivation for me that made me untouchable. Nothing was going to stop me; nothing was going to get in the way of making my family proud. If my mother put her life on the line for me, I was willing to put my life on the line for her. Ever since the dark months in 2010, my drive to succeed in school and soccer was on a whole other level. My decisions weren't about me anymore; it was about my family. In life, as my role model Inky Johnson said, "If every decision and choice you make is just about you, you're going to hit something that's a lot tougher than you and it's going to make you quit because you don't have a driving force for why you do what you do." But when you find a bigger purpose to why you do what you do, you become unstoppable, because you're serving something bigger than yourself and a human being with drive and motivation is a machine.

I took away many lessons in life from this experience. Tomorrow is never promised to anyone, and we should never take the gift of today for granted because someone, somewhere, is fighting for their tomorrow. The Dalai Lama once said, "There are only two days in the year that nothing can be done. One is called yesterday and the other is called tomorrow, so today is the right day to love, believe, do, and mostly live." What you put off for tomorrow may never get finished, because life is too precious. We should all respect the saying, "Now or never." If you love someone, hold them tight, never let them go, and tell them that you love them because you never know when they can be gone.

"How tragic that man can never realize how beautiful life is until he is face to face with death."

-Ikiru

I didn't realize how precious life truly was until I saw my mother almost lose hers. I personally believe that the moment you encounter death is the moment you start to live. You start to realize that all the small accidents, arguments, and failures you encounter are nothing compared to the grand scheme of things. You start to see how none of us have an infinite amount of time on this Earth, and you start making moves that you've always wanted to do because of this vision.

The college degree you wanted, now is the time to go get it.

The particular job you wanted, now is the time to go get it.

The city you've always wanted to visit; now is the time to go.

That special person you met, now is the right time to go tell them that you love them.

The dream you had, now is the time to go after it.

Life is too precious.

CHAPTER 6:

———————— ❧❧❧❧❧ ————————

LETTING GO

"Sometimes holding on does more

damage than letting go."

I always dreamed of dating this girl in my Chemistry class during my junior year of high school Cleveland. She was absolutely gorgeous, and I always wanted to be in her group during lab projects. One day, I heard rumors going around the school that she liked me too! This was almost a dream come true. We started talking towards the end of my junior year, which was her sophomore year of high school. I still remember our first date to the movies; I surprised her with roses, and she was amazed because she had never been treated like that. We started dating soon after and everything was a dream come true for us. I would spend every possible moment with her and talk to her on the phone every night until either one of us fell asleep. The summer of 2015, I went to Japan for 2 weeks to go see my family, and we thought it was the end of the world for us because we had never gone even 2 days without seeing each other. Everything was going perfect for us, there was nothing but happiness and both of our parents loved us being together and supported us through it all. We had our entire lives planned out, where we were going to get married, where we were going to live, how many kids we were going to have, and even their names. We were in love.

As I was going off to college at the University of Louisville, we were confident in the long-distance relationship. However, things started getting difficult for us. When there is no physical presence, the only way to build trust is through communication, and I would change my sleep schedule just to be able to talk to her. However, preseason at Louisville was tough, and the lack of sleep played a crucial role in my first season with the Cardinals. I kept getting injured and tore my quadriceps muscle 4 days before the season opener, which was heartbreaking for me and my family. I can never blame anyone for my injuries, but the small things may have added up. As a senior in high school, she was constantly worried about what I was doing, and I understood her perspective. Things kept getting more difficult for us. We started arguing when I would go out to dinner with my teammates or go hang out with my friends, because she felt insecure. This was also my fault, because I made her feel insecure. As she went off to college at the Ohio State

University, things got even more difficult because we had different values. I was a student-athlete, so I didn't live the "ordinary" college student life of constantly going out and drinking, but she enjoyed her free time, which I respected. However, our differences in values really started separating us to the point where we broke up after two and a half years. I was absolutely heartbroken.

We both tried so hard to hang on, but there was nothing left to hang on to. Being in love with someone to becoming complete strangers is one of the hardest things to do. This was a moment I never imagined, because I really thought that we were going to get married and live a happy life. But like I said, sometimes holding on does more damage than letting go. As time went on, I got to spend more time alone and it made me realize that maybe breaking up was the right thing to do because we were both holding each other back from our career paths. We were trying so hard to not let go of our relationship that our individual journeys of me trying to become a professional soccer player and her trying to become a registered nurse were slowly getting distant because our focus was on each other. We were both struggling individually at that time, as I was struggling in soccer and she was struggling in school. Although I was heartbroken when we broke up, I got to work on my individual goals and get back on track, which was very important to me and my family. Sometimes, even though you may be distracted by the relationship you are in, it is important to look at your life from a broader perspective because nothing is permanent except for who you are. I am beyond thankful for the two and a half years that I got to spend with her, because she not only gave me memories that I will cherish for the rest of my life, but because she shaped me into the man I am now. Going through a difficult breakup is important because it teaches people to be wiser, patient, and tough, three things that only life can teach you.

During a breakup, it is important to understand that there is no easy way out; it will be painful, and it will take time. But it is important to understand that there is a rainbow waiting after the storm, which means that once you get over the sad times, you will be in peace. It is so important to let your emotions out. Don't try to keep them bottled in because you have to release what's inside of you sometimes. It is okay to cry and feel weak, that is the only way you will become strong. I also believe that you must surround yourself with people you love and trust, like family and friends. Being around such people helps you get your mind off your significant other to simply enjoy the present moment. Don't try to bounce back from a break up by getting in to another relationship right away.

You won't be ready; your heart's just been broken, and forcing yourself to get into another relationship won't help you become happier. It is important to be patient and understand that God's timing is perfect.

"If you ask God to send you someone who you deserve, don't be surprised if it takes a while. Before he delivers what you want, you first have to become the person capable of being in that relationship. Until then, he will just prepare while he monitors your growth."

You can't rush something you want forever.

CHAPTER 7:

⚘⚘⚘

DREAMS OF REALITY

"Nobody is taller than

the last man standing."

As long as you don't give up, you keep your dream alive; and that is so important. I was born into a soccer family, spending my Saturday nights in the locker-room of Kashiwa Reysol's (professional soccer team in Japan) home stadium, while my father was working on the field as a professional trainer. I was always surrounded by professional soccer players, which ignited my passion for the sport. I started playing soccer when I was 3-years-old with my father and brother, and I have dreamed of playing professional soccer ever since. We were constantly moving from city to city, so I didn't have a lot of friends. My only friend was the soccer ball, and I became obsessed with the sport. On Christmas one year, Santa gifted me a baseball bat and a baseball glove which my father threw out in the garbage the very next day because he did not let my brother or I play any other sport. I loved copying my brother. Whatever he did, I did too, and I think that's where I learned all of my soccer skills, because he is my role model. When we moved to Cleveland, our apartment had a racquetball court and my family would spend hours every night playing soccer there until we got kicked out by the manager, which were some of my favorite memories. I started out playing locally in a neighborhood league and, year by year, I started getting noticed. I eventually made my way up to the highest tier of youth soccer in the United States, the United States Soccer Development Academy. Before any colleges started reaching out to me, I knew I was only going to go to the University of Louisville or the University of Akron, two of the best college soccer programs in the nation. I took an offer from the University of Louisville without any hesitation and started my NCAA career in 2016.

This was my first time being away from my parents, and I was definitely homesick for the first few weeks. I wasn't mentally mature enough either and did not play to my full potential during preseason. I was constantly getting injured and ended up redshirting my freshman year at Louisville. During my sophomore year, I was playing with fear and did not meet my coach's expectations, which forced me to spend most of my time on the bench. Back to back years, I hit an all-time low in my soccer career, which made me frustrated and depressed. After my redshirt freshman season at Louisville, I decided to transfer to the University of Akron, another soccer powerhouse. I knew this was another opportunity for me to change the environment before the environment changed me. As I slowly started getting my confidence back, I was getting happier and happier with my play. However, I had some disagreements with the coaching staff and wasn't given too many opportunities to show my capabilities. However, I knew that as long as I didn't give up on my goals, I would give myself an opportunity. In September 2018, when I was in midseason with Akron, I got a 3-month trial offer from a professional team in Santa Catarina, Brazil, through the Japanese Football Association.

"Take the first step in faith. You don't have to see the whole staircase, just take the first step."

-Dr. Martin Luther King Jr.

As a 20-year-old who didn't know a lick of Portuguese, or even where the Joinville Esporte Clube was, I took my first leap of faith. During the 3-month trial, the head coach of the first team was bought by another team, so the new coach that came in arrived 3 weeks before my departure. This meant I had 3 weeks to show the coach what I had been doing since I was 3-years-old. After the first week, I pulled my right hamstring and was heartbroken because I knew my chance was gone. However, my parents told me, "Kota, this is your last chance of becoming a professional soccer player, you can regret giving up or fight through it." Instead of sitting out for the next two weeks, I played with a pulled hamstring. I had never experienced so much pain and fear in my life, but I knew I had to keep going no matter what the circumstances. After the three weeks, I was offered a one-year professional contract and became the first ever Professional-Asian athlete to come through the city of Joinville, Brazil.

God really does have a plan.

The strongest power we, as human beings, hold is the power of not giving up. As long as you don't give up, you will always give yourself an opportunity. At the same time, we must realize that just because we don't give up does not mean we will reach the destination we dreamed of. The journey is more important than the destination, and if you don't enjoy the journey, you will most likely not enjoy the destination. With the right perspective, failure is a blessing in disguise because it teaches you lessons you can't learn anywhere else in life. I personally have failed more times than I have succeeded, whether that may be in school, soccer, or life in general. However, without the failures that I have encountered, I would not be who I am today. It is tremendously difficult to see failure from a positive perspective because no one likes to fail, but being able to use failure as a stepping stone for the next chapter of your life is a technique we are all capable of learning. After a bad practice or a bad game, I like to write down what I did wrong and think of ways in which I can improve the next time. This is simply because I'm not competing with other teams or other players in my position, I'm competing with myself, and as long as I can be better than who I was the day before, I am where I need to be. That is life.

Soccer has taught me many lessons that I will carry for the rest of my life. One of the most important lessons I learned as an athlete was that when a problem occurred during a game or practice, I couldn't hide from it and wait for someone else to take care of it. Instead, I had to solve the problem in the moment or else I was going to jeopardize the entire game or practice. So, when I encounter trials and tribulations in life, I cannot run away from them. I must face them and solve the situation immediately, which I think is very important.

Everything in life is impossible until someone does it. If you are waiting for your chance to go after what you want, you will never catch it. You must go out there and create your own chance. If not now, when? If not me, who?

CHAPTER 8:

———————— ❧ ————————

WE ARE WHO WE ARE

There were twenty minutes left in the second half with the game tied at 1-1 after I scored the opening goal for us. My teammate made a successful defensive play to win the ball back. As we were coming down the field on offense, the coach of the opposing team screamed, "Don't let the Chinese kid get the ball!" as it was easier for him to describe me by my appearance rather than the Number 10 on my jersey. I was crushed. I couldn't play in the game anymore, and I was subbed off as I held my tears back on the bench in a U-13 travel soccer game.

Racism was something my family and I had struggled with while living in the United States—my father nearly lost his job every year because of his race and his inability to fluently speak English. Little do my father's superiors know of the sacrifices he had made to get to where he was and the sacrifices he continued to make—waking up at 5:30 am every day to get to the hospital an hour early to read every up on the medical history of the patients he would be seeing that day and working overtime to complete his dictation even after everyone had left. His work ethic and dedication to be the best in what he did was unmatched, yet his job was always on the line because of his "inability."

My father wasn't the only one facing the brunt of racism, my brother was a victim too. After one of his indoor soccer games, my brother stayed back to practice by himself off the field, *not in the way of the game that was going on*. Then, out of nowhere, an old white man came up to my brother.

"Get out of the way! This isn't China. You can't play wherever," the old man shouted.

"You can't say that!" My brother was shocked.

But the man ignored my brother and refused to apologize for what he had said, adding, "You're distracting us. That's why we're losing."

The playing team then asked the referee to kick my brother out, but he refused to leave, waiting for an apology with a broken heart.

During my freshman year in high school, I took a mentoring class where we talked about goal-setting. As a task, we had to complete the following sentence: "After high school, I want to..." I wrote that I wanted "to play Division 1 soccer at one of the top ten schools in the country." My teacher kicked me out of class, saying my goal wasn't realistic.

As a Japanese-American, I have always been told who I am or who should be—whether I'm supposed to be good at math, know how to play the piano, go to college to become a doctor, if my mom works at a nail salon, or if my family owns an Asian restaurant. I've even been told that I don't belong—in the United States or in Brazil.

Being the first professional Asian athlete to play for Joinville Esporte Clube, I've received a lot of love, but even more hatred. I've been told by our fans and the people of Joinville that people of my ethnicity shouldn't play soccer, that the fans will never pay money to watch a Japanese kid play, that I wouldn't be able to keep up with Brazilian soccer, that Joinville was wasting money on me, and that I don't belong here, so I should go home. I realized that doing what others say you should is the easiest thing to do, but doing what they say you can't is the hardest. The only person that can hold you back is yourself. We are limitless.

From a young boy troubled by the vagaries of racism to an adult who is conscious of his own self-worth. I'm so thankful to have experienced so many racial conflicts during my 21 years of life because it has allowed me to understand that what I think about myself matters more than the opinion of strangers. I have learned to love and appreciate myself.

Attempt the impossible because that's the only way you can make it possible.

I took the hits, and I'll continue to take hits, but I will never allow myself to be defeated. I'll continue to rise up every single time because if I don't, I'll make it that much harder for the future generations of Asians, blacks, Hispanics, Middle-Easterners, gays, and, most importantly, my kids—kids I hope to have in the future, to see light in the dark. I am who I am, and I won't ever change myself for the world.

Whenever life overwhelms me, I keep the Serenity Prayer close to me because it has helped me find the solution in every problem and the importance of self-control. It says, "God, grant me the serenity to accept the things I cannot change, courage to change the things I can, and wisdom to know the difference."

I can't control what other people say or think about me. I can only control how I react to it. When I was younger, racist comments used to hurt me, holding me back from engaging in several activities because I have been told that I did not belong in certain environments. But as I grew older, I realized that these people who make racially offensive comments know nothing about me. At the end of the day, I am the one walking in my shoes—not someone else—so I'll never let the opinion of others affect me. The moment I show weakness is the moment I let racism win, which is something that our world still struggles with. People tend to highlight differences among each other based on aspects they can't control, such as the color of their skin or their ethnicity because they feel as if certain race or ethnicity is superior to others. But the moment we learn to love ourselves for who we are and realize that racially controversial remarks or hatred from some people don't define who we are, but who they are, we take a step closer toward putting an end to racism. I personally believe that racism and hatred stemming from it will still continue long after I die, and so I consider it my duty to make the lives of future generations much easier in this aspect by sharing my personal experiences.

We are all human beings at the end of the day, having more things in common than not. So there is no reason to show hate when we can show love.

I'm a proud Japanese-American citizen. I'm proud of my background, and I'm beyond thankful for my family. I'll continue to embrace my culture and spread love. And to anyone who has experienced racism or found it difficult to love themselves, I would like to say that everything will heal. *I'm With You.*

Made in the USA
Las Vegas, NV
07 November 2022

58998853R00042